SPARK

Jim West's Electrifying Adventures in
Creating the Microphone

For Alex and Lena, so that they can see themselves in this world, too
AR

To my father, Albert, and my mother, Matilda—
who taught me to dream big and work diligently. Thank you!
SF

SPARK

Jim West's Electrifying Adventures
in Creating the Microphone

Ainissa Ramirez

illustrated by Setor Fiadzigbey

mit Kids Press

JIM WEST'S brain was crowded with questions. On his grandmother's Virginia farm, he could be found by the well, under the house, or on a branch. His imagination was quick like lightning. Every five minutes he had a new idea. But no one around him seemed to appreciate them.

When Jim was indoors and couldn't move around, all those questions bubbling inside of him began to build. It didn't take long before they burst out of him.

How did his toy work?
How did his little brother's toy work?
How did his grandfather's pocket watch tick?

    Often, he got answers to those questions with help from his screwdriver. Whenever an adult found something disassembled in the house, it wasn't long before Jim heard a voice calling out his name. A punishment was coming. It happened every time. Even so, he had to know how things worked.

One August day while Jim was out walking, he saw an old radio that someone had thrown out. He grabbed it and rushed home.

Inside the radio lived a nest of wires, a skyline of vacuum tubes, and a cone that vibrated in and out to make sounds.

Jim tinkered and searched for how to fix it.

Then he bounced onto the bed holding the frayed cord. When he plugged it in . . .

Electricity zipped through the cord to his hand to his arm to his chest to his feet to the bedpost and then to the floor. He couldn't get his fingers to let go.

His older brother saw him and pushed him off the bed.

Afterward, Jim said he wasn't scared. He learned electricity had done this to him. Now he had to know all about it.

His aunt Dorothy gave him a book about electricity. Jim read that his new hero, Ben Franklin, flew a kite in a storm. Franklin figured out that clouds were full of electric charge and, when they couldn't hold any more, lightning flashed out of them.

Jim asked his grandmother if he could fly a kite in a storm, too. Of course, she told him it was too dangerous. He listened to her, but this didn't stop him from daydreaming about flying a kite under the crackle of lightning one day.

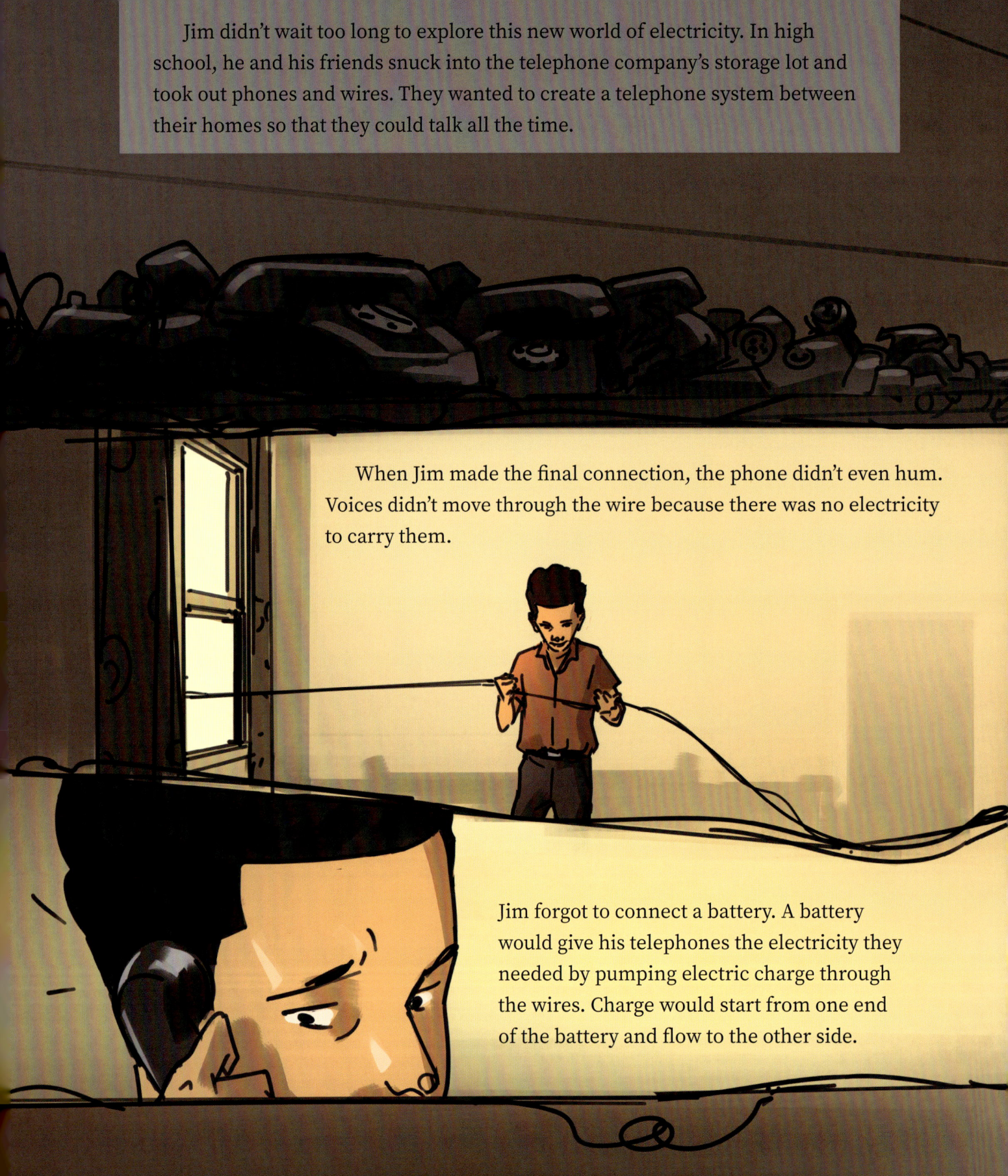

Jim didn't wait too long to explore this new world of electricity. In high school, he and his friends snuck into the telephone company's storage lot and took out phones and wires. They wanted to create a telephone system between their homes so that they could talk all the time.

When Jim made the final connection, the phone didn't even hum. Voices didn't move through the wire because there was no electricity to carry them.

Jim forgot to connect a battery. A battery would give his telephones the electricity they needed by pumping electric charge through the wires. Charge would start from one end of the battery and flow to the other side.

But before Jim could install a battery, the telephone company found out. His father ordered him to take those wires down.

With thoughts of electricity zipping through his mind, Jim told his parents he wanted to go to college to study science.

They tried to talk him out of it because they felt that it was impossible for an African American to work as a scientist.

His parents had seen this firsthand.

Jim's mother studied math. At the Langley Aeronautical Laboratory, she used big calculators to figure out flight paths and space orbits. But she was fired when her bosses discovered that outside of work she was also a civil rights organizer.

Jim's father was a Pullman porter for the railroad and knew three Black chemists who had to work as mailmen because no laboratory would hire them.

Jim's father told him that if he wanted to study science, he would have to do it on his own. His father wouldn't pay for it.

Studying science was Jim's dream. His parents wanted him to forget it. He couldn't. He loved it too much. His dream was bigger than all those negatives. Jim left Virginia and headed to college in Philadelphia.

In his science classes, he was one of only two Black students.

He saved money by staying with distant relatives and earned money by repairing broken televisions.

While at school, Jim saw an ad for a summer job at Bell Labs, the home of inventions like gadgets for telephones and computer parts called transistors.

At Bell Labs, he'd be encouraged to take things apart, unlike when he was a boy back in Virginia.

Jim got the job!

The Bell Labs scientists had a project for him. They created headphones, but the sound coming out was too quiet. These headphones would be of no use for their experiments unless Jim could fix them.

Jim didn't know much about headphones, so he dashed to the library and read lots of books. This gave him an idea.

Jim drew a plastic drum with a slice of metal next to it. He had to figure out how to make the drum move in and out. These vibrations would make a sound.

He knew that opposite charges moved toward each other and charges that were the same moved apart. His plan was to use electricity to give charge to the drum and give the metal the opposite charge.

He learned that if he kept changing the charge of the metal and made it sometimes the same as the drum and sometimes the opposite, the drum would move away from the metal and then move closer.

When the plastic drum moved in and out like that, those vibrations would make a sound.

That's how his headphones would work!

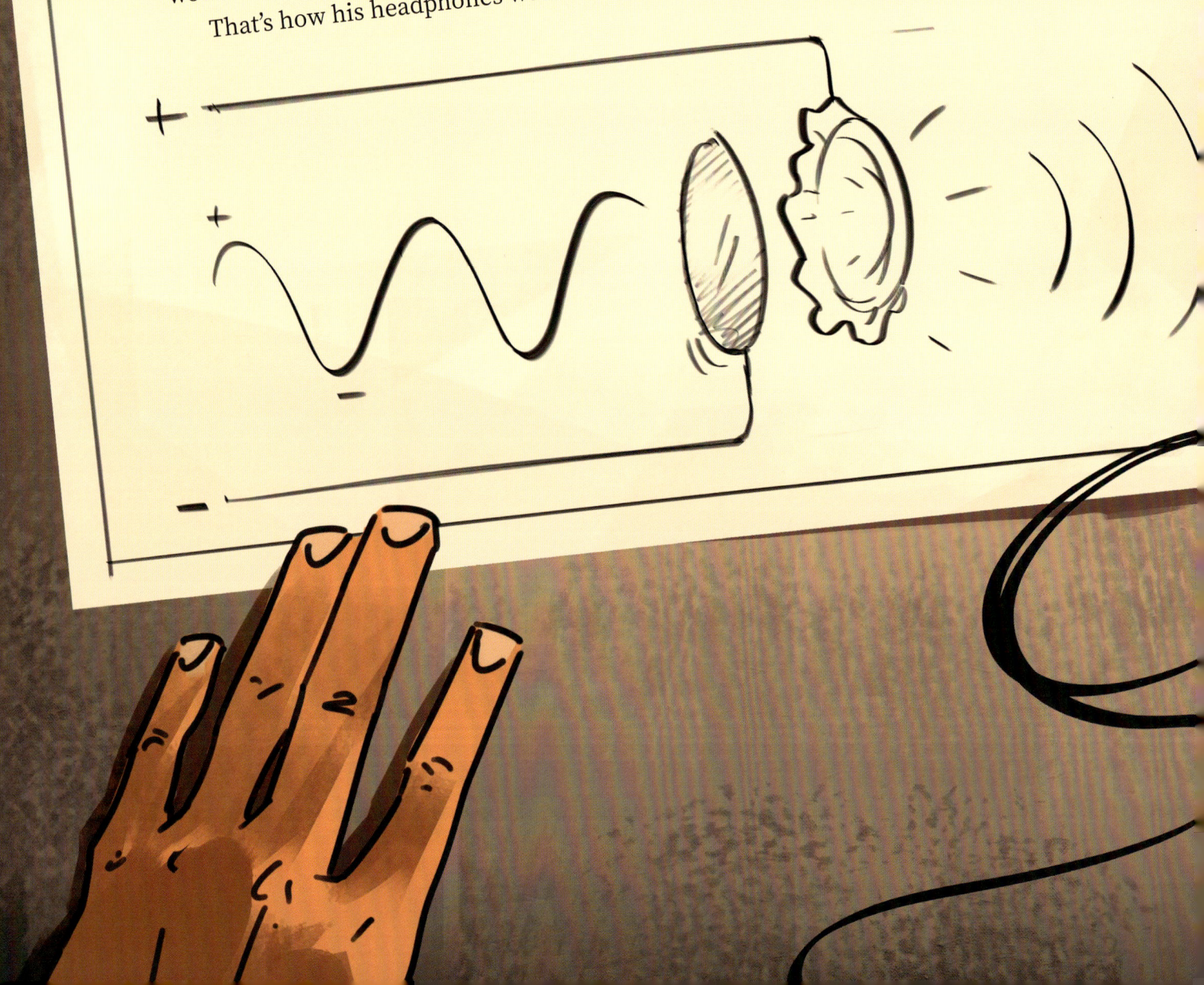

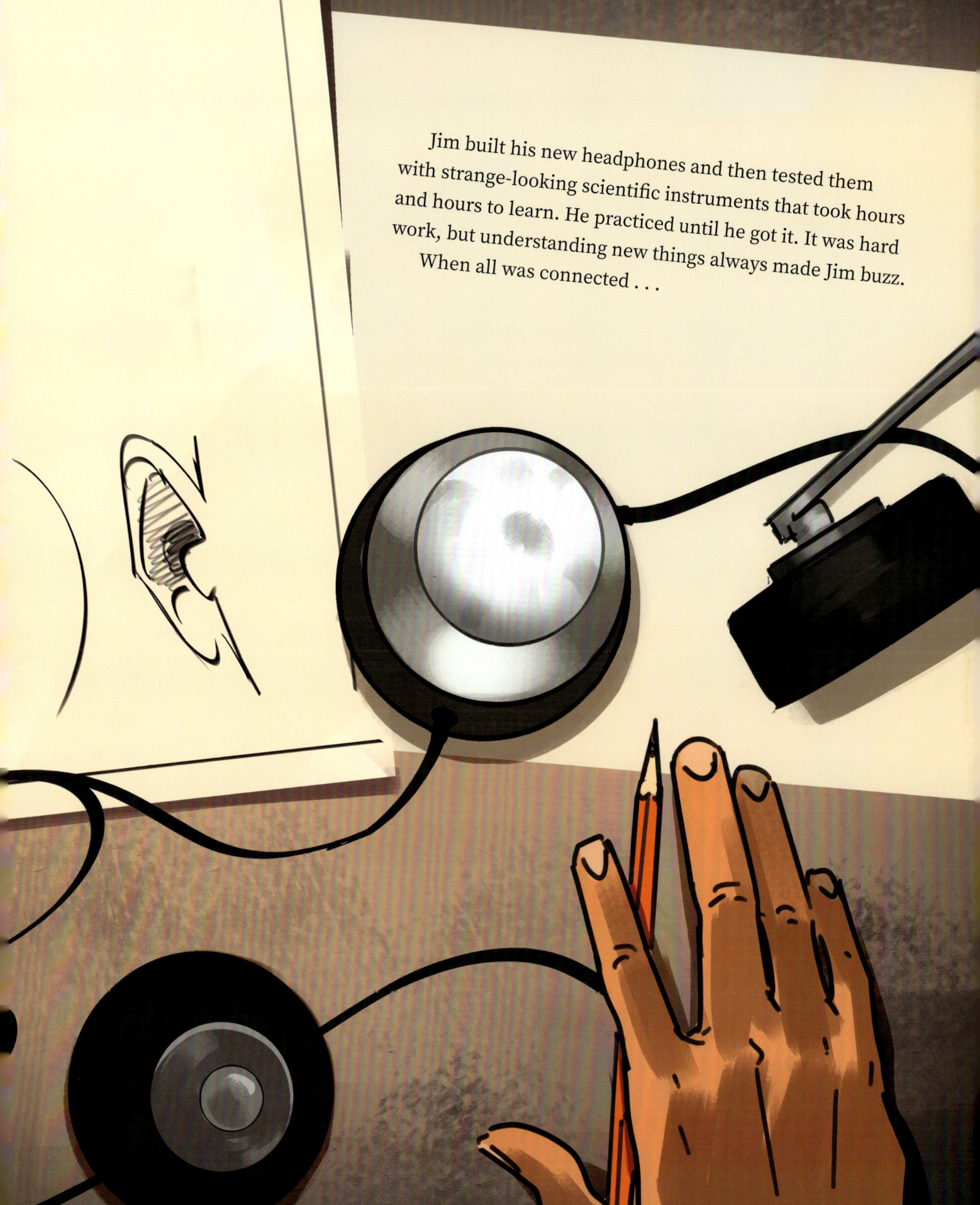

Jim built his new headphones and then tested them with strange-looking scientific instruments that took hours and hours to learn. He practiced until he got it. It was hard work, but understanding new things always made Jim buzz. When all was connected . . .

It worked!

Bell Labs was the playground Jim always wanted. Not only did it have new things to discover, but it also had people to discover with. Jim saw Black scientists. There were others who looked like him, and they loved science, too. He finally found a place where he belonged. So when the summer ended and his time there was done, going back to school in Philadelphia wasn't his favorite thought.

That fall, Jim's boss from Bell Labs called him at school. The headphones he created were now quiet, too. Jim scratched his head and told his boss he would try to fix them. With that, they sent him a train ticket.

Jim tinkered and searched for what was wrong. He took the headphones apart. He tested the electrical circuit. He made sure that electricity could flow through all the wires. He also checked that the plastic drum and the metal were getting the electrical charges they needed. When he turned everything on, the plastic drum vibrated and made a loud beep again.

One time, he accidentally pulled out a wire. The electricity stopped flowing. But his headphones sang out with a . . .

BEEEEEEP!

"That's funny!"

It shouldn't do that without electricity!

A light bulb needs electricity to work. Shouldn't his headphones?

Jim realized the plastic in the drum didn't need electricity to give it charge, because it was full of its own charge already. It was acting like Ben Franklin's storm cloud!

Jim rushed back to the library to find a book that listed materials that held electric charge. The plastic he used was one. Jim read that it was like a storm cloud, except it was a bit different. The plastic didn't let go of its charge the way a cloud did with lightning. The plastic kept its charge for years and years. That's why his headphones worked.

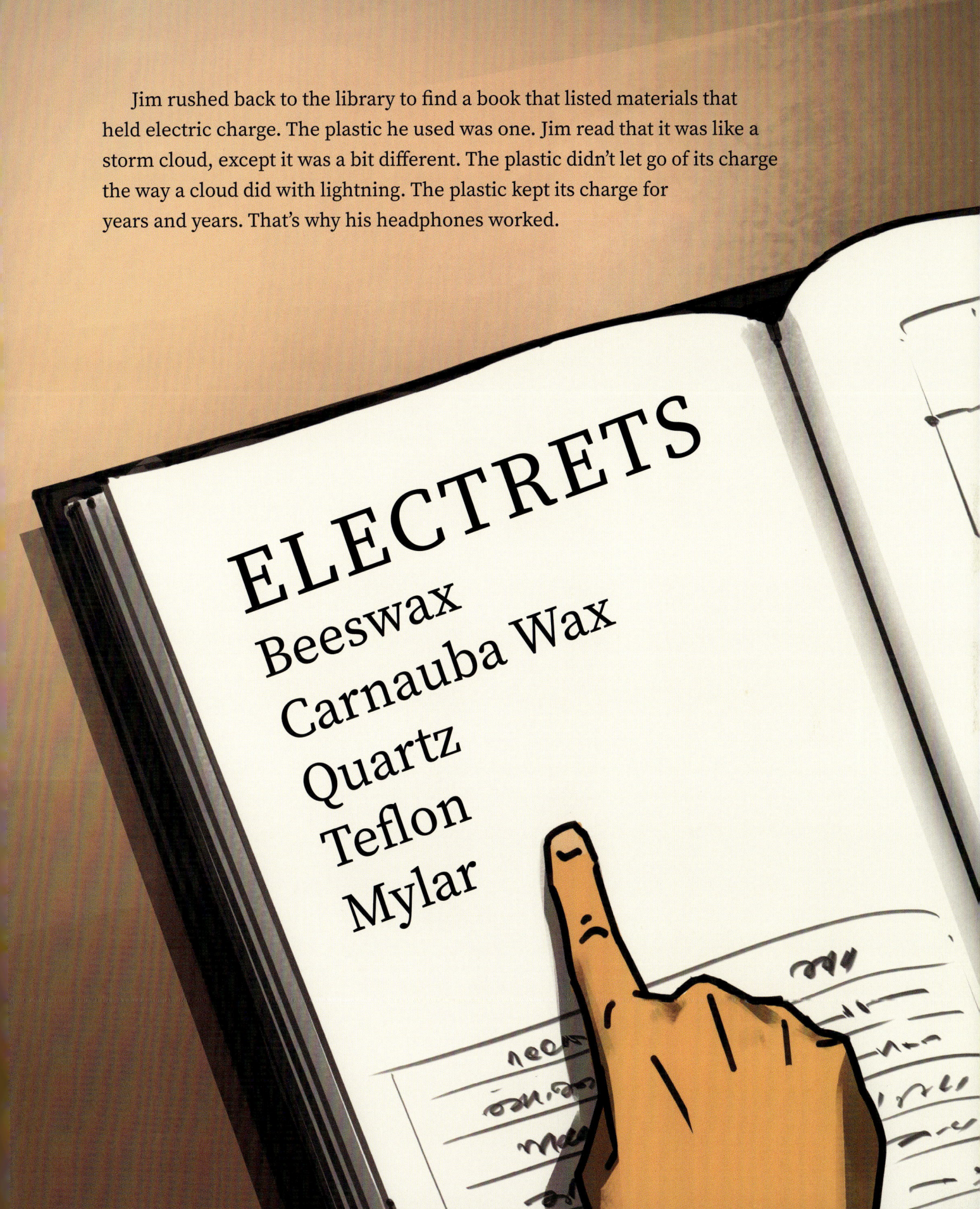

ELECTRETS
Beeswax
Carnauba Wax
Quartz
Teflon
Mylar

Jim was buzzing with questions. He had one that was the biggest. If this material could make sounds like a mouth, could it also hear sounds like an ear? Jim wanted to make a microphone. He knew that microphones acted like headphones in reverse.

Jim ran back to the lab to find out. He tinkered and then spoke into the plastic drum. His voice sent vibrations through the air that made the drum vibrate up and down. When the drum moved up and down, the circuit gave off an electrical signal that went up and down, too. He turned his voice into electricity.

His new microphone worked!

Jim was bursting with other ideas. He teamed up with Gerhard Sessler, who also worked on microphones. Together they tested how well this new microphone picked up . . .

soft sounds in the world's quietest room . . .

loud bands
in auditoriums . . .

and low rumbles
from a distant rocket's
boom.

Microphones in old telephones made people sound like they had a sore throat. But with Jim West's microphones, voices were crystal clear. Plus, his microphones could be made smaller than a button, because they didn't need big electrical parts to charge them.

Soon, everyone saw how wonderful his invention was. It wasn't long before his microphones were used everywhere from toys to computers to cell phones.

When Jim West was young, no one back on that farm in Virginia approved of how he behaved or appreciated where his curiosity took him. But just a few years later, it was that same curiosity that created his wonderful microphone, which changed how the whole wide world communicates.

AUTHOR'S NOTE

I HAD THE DISTINCT PLEASURE of meeting Jim West when I was a newly minted scientist at Bell Labs in Murray Hill, New Jersey. He was kind enough to meet me for lunch in the cafeteria. I don't remember what we talked about, but I do remember that I felt like I was in the presence of a great man. Decades later, after the movie *Hidden Figures* came out, I realized that there were many more Black inventors who made contributions to science and remained unknown to most people. It also dawned on me that I had met one! So I reached out to Jim West again, and he agreed to speak with me. In our conversations, he shared with me a wealth of science knowledge, but he also had advice on how to navigate the world. It was a great honor to spend time with him.

My hope is that I captured his greatness, his spirit, and his tenacity, as well as the lessons I learned: He taught me it was important to remain curious. He taught me to not let anything get in the way of my curiosity. He also taught me to not let anyone define me. We live in a world that often squelches curiosity and individuality. That is why it is important to have a role model like Jim West.

ACKNOWLEDGMENTS

MANY THANKS TO JIM WEST and Gerhard Sessler for their time, knowledge, and generosity. Thanks also go to Sheldon Hochheiser (AT&T Archives) and Chris Hunter (Museum of Innovation and Science) for their valuable resources.

THE LIFE AND WORK OF JIM WEST

James Edward Maceo West was born February 10, 1931, in Farmville, Virginia, a small southern town located about sixty miles west of Richmond. He lived in a house his grandfather built, with his mother, his father, his uncle, his grandmother, and his younger brother, Nate. (Jim also had an older half-brother who lived in another house.) When Jim was about thirteen years old, his mother moved the family to Hampton, Virginia, which was a city with a better high school for Black students. While there, Jim's mother worked at NACA's Langley Aeronautical Laboratory (which is now NASA's Langley Research Center). She performed mathematical calculations there, like the women depicted in the movie *Hidden Figures*.

When Jim was a little boy, he was notorious for taking things apart and for getting into lots of trouble. His energy and curiosity were hard to tame. What was clear to everyone back then was that he was a very bright boy. It was for this reason that when Jim was growing up, his family hoped that he would be a medical doctor. Jim's uncle was the local dentist, and everyone wished that Jim would have a practice next door to his uncle's office. But Jim liked physics better than medicine and told his parents that he wanted to study physics in college. They were against this idea. Jim enrolled anyway, even though he didn't have their support.

At first, he attended Hampton Institute, in Virginia. Later, he transferred to Temple University, in Philadelphia, and applied for a summer internship at Bell Labs. At Bell Labs, he worked in a department full of psychoacousticians, or scientists who study how people perceive sound. These scientists wanted to determine the shortest time between two beeps that could be detected by the human ear. They needed very good headphones to do these experiments.

Jim West designed them and inadvertently discovered a unique (but old) type of material called an electret that allowed the headphones to work when he accidentally disconnected them from a source of electricity.

Electrets had been a scientific curiosity for a long time because, unlike most other materials, they store charge and keep their electric charge permanently. The electret that Jim West initially used was a plastic called Mylar, which is commonly used today for helium party balloons. After Jim discovered the electret nature of the material in his headphones, he then decided to see whether this material could be used for a microphone. He teamed up with fellow scientist Gerhard Sessler, and they created what is called the foil-electret microphone, which was granted a patent in 1964 (US Patent 3,118,022). They used a better-performing electret material, called Teflon, which is also used as a coating in nonstick pans today. What makes this invention so unique is that the material doesn't need to be connected to a source of power to work. As such, these microphones can be made very, very small. While these microphones were first envisioned to be used in landline telephones, they took off in other electronics such as tape recorders, hearing aids, cell phones, toys, tablets, computers, and other gadgets. Over two billion of these microphones are made every year!

For this work, Jim West was inducted into the National Inventors Hall of Fame in 1999. In 2006, he was awarded the National Medal of Technology and Innovation, and he won the Benjamin Franklin Medal in 2010. He was also the president of the Acoustical Society of America from 1998 to 1999. Jim West made significant strides in science but also in increasing the number of scientists of color. At Bell Labs, he began a program for students to have summer internships. Many young people have benefited from this program, and society has benefited from all the inventions they have created. Jim West left a mark not only with his incredible invention but also by opening doors for others.

TIME LINE

THE ROAD TO THE INVENTION of the microphone was a long one. It took effort from all parts of the world. Every culture has a means to communicate. The microphone is just one of them.

ANCIENT TIMES	Ancient peoples all over the world use bells, drums, fire, mirrors, and smoke signals to communicate with each other.
1664	Robert Hooke creates the cup-and-string telephone in England.
1752	Benjamin Franklin proves lightning is electricity with a kite experiment.
1792	In France, the Chappe brothers create a flag-and-pole system for sending messages, called semaphore.
1832	Samuel F. B. Morse conceives of the idea of a telegraph. William Cooke and Charles Wheatstone create a telegraph in England.
1844	Samuel F. B. Morse sends the first official telegraph message ("What hath God wrought") from Baltimore to Washington, DC.
1876	Alexander Graham Bell patents his telephone.

1877	Emile Berliner makes an early microphone.
	Thomas Edison patents a speaking telegraph.
1884	Granville T. Woods, an African American inventor, patents a telephone transmitter, or microphone (US Patent 308,817).
1892	In England, Oliver Heaviside coins the term *electret*.
1920	Edward C. Wente designs a modern telephone transmitter, or microphone.
1928	In Japan, Mototaro Eguchi makes a modern wax-electret microphone.
1942	William Bruno sells a wax-electret microphone.
1962	Jim West and Gerhard Sessler publish their first paper on their foil-electret microphone.
1964	Jim West and Gerhard Sessler are awarded a patent for the electroacoustic transducer, or microphone (US Patent 3,118,002).
TODAY	Billions of foil-electret microphones are used by people all over the world.

MORE ABOUT JIM WEST

LISTEN to Jim West

West, James. "James West on Invention and Inclusion in Science."
Interview by Madeline K. Sofia. *Short Wave*, NPR, February 23, 2021. Audio, 13:40.
https://www.npr.org/2021/02/22/970159013/james-west-on-invention-and-inclusion-in-science.

SEE Jim West

West, James. "The HistoryMakers Video Oral History Interview with James West."
Interview by The HistoryMakers. February 13, 2013. Video, 3:29:20.
https://www.thehistorymakers.org/biography/james-west.

LEARN about Jim West

Simpson, Joanne Cavanaugh. "Sound Reasoning."
Johns Hopkins Magazine, September 2003.
https://pages.jh.edu/jhumag/0903web/west.html.

READ about Jim West's Invention

Lemelson–MIT. "Gerhard Sessler and James West: Foil Electret Microphone."
https://lemelson.mit.edu/resources/gerhard-sessler-and-james-west.

FIND Jim West's Patent

Sessler, Gerhard, and James West. Electroacoustic transducer.
US Patent 3,118,022 A, filed May 22, 1962, and issued January 14, 1964.
https://patents.google.com/patent/US3118022A/en.

Ainissa Ramirez dreamed of becoming a scientist when she was a little girl. She got the idea after seeing an African American girl solve problems on a television show called *3-2-1 Contact*. In that moment, she saw her reflection. She later earned her doctorate in materials science from Stanford and worked at Bell Labs, where she met Jim West. She wrote this book so that others can see their reflections in science, too.

Setor Fiadzigbey is an illustrator, artist, art director, and concept artist. Originally from Ghana, he studied science and engineering before realizing he wanted to be an artist. Since then, he has illustrated *Nic Blake and the Remarkables* by Angie Thomas, *Bunheads* by Misty Copeland, and *Epic Athletes: LeBron James* by Dan Wetzel.

The MIT Press, the ≡mit Kids Press colophon, and MIT Kids Press are trademarks of The MIT Press,
a department of the Massachusetts Institute of Technology, and used under license from The MIT Press.
The colophon and MIT Kids Press are registered in the US Patent and Trademark Office.

First edition 2025

Library of Congress Catalog Card Number pending
ISBN 978-1-5362-2528-0

25 26 27 28 29 30 CCP 10 9 8 7 6 5 4 3 2 1

Printed in Shenzhen, Guangdong, China

This book was typeset in Source Serif.
The illustrations were created digitally.

MIT Kids Press
an imprint of Candlewick Press
99 Dover Street
Somerville, Massachusetts 02144

mitkidspress.com
candlewick.com

EU Authorized Representative: HackettFlynn Ltd., 36 Cloch Choirneal, Balrothery,
Co. Dublin, K32 C942, Ireland. EU@walkerpublishinggroup.com